# EXCELLENCE FOR ACTORS

PSYCHOLOGY FOR ACTORS SERIES

ALEXA ISPAS

ISBN: 978-1-913926-27-4 (pbk)

ISBN: 978-1-913926-26-7 (ebk)

# CONTENTS

# INTRODUCTION

We all know that becoming a great actor requires hard work, but how do you achieve excellence in your craft?

What actions do you take to reach your full potential?

Perhaps you have spent years taking acting classes without any noticeable improvement.

Or maybe your acting improved for a while, but you don't know how to make further progress.

This lack of clarity is likely to lead to dissatisfaction and a decline in your enthusiasm for the craft.

After all, nobody goes into acting aiming for mediocrity.

If this sounds familiar, psychology can help.

For many years, psychologists have been studying how those dedicated to their craft achieve mastery.

The biggest reveal of this exploration has been "deliberate practice," a process through which you turn a laser-like focus on small, measurable areas of improvement.

This type of practice leads to noticeable and inevitable progress when used consistently.

The benefits of deliberate practice have been explored by research on "high achievers"–people who have reached the top in their chosen field, including athletes, musicians, and chess masters.

This research has shown that using deliberate practice makes it possible to reach your full potential, irrespective of talent or other inborn abilities.

Can deliberate practice help actors in the same way?

If so, how would you apply the principles of deliberate practice to acting?

In *Excellence for Actors*, the first book to explore deliberate practice in the context of the acting craft, you will gain a new level of clarity over how to reach your full potential.

As you will learn, achieving excellence is not just about working hard.

It is also about focusing your efforts and time on goals that lead to real and measurable progress.

Throughout this book, we will explore deliberate practice and discuss how to apply it to the acting craft.

We will also discuss how to ensure your commitment to deliberate practice is sustainable by making certain mindset and lifestyle adjustments.

There are many great books about the acting craft, such as those that teach the intricacies of a particular technique.

This book is about something more fundamental: the process of working on your craft, irrespective of any technique you may use.

I have kept this book short, so you can read it in an afternoon and gain access to all the tools you need to pursue excellence as an actor.

# CHAPTER 1

# A CLEAR PATH TO EXCELLENCE

## A NEED FOR CLARITY

Gaining clarity over how to make progress in your craft is difficult as an actor.

There are many areas where you could improve.

This may include audition technique, voice work, mastering particular accents, or learning new skills, such as playing the piano.

How do you decide where to focus your efforts?

To reassure yourself that you are doing something, you may take on lots of acting-related activities and spread yourself thin, with no clarity over how your actions will lead to progress.

You may end up spending time and money on various classes, coaching sessions, and subscriptions, hoping that something will stick and that your efforts will make you a better actor.

The problem is that if you only set the vague goal of "getting better," but are not working towards something concrete, you cannot remain consistent.

As such, making meaningful progress in any particular area is impossible.

All this frenetic and unfocused activity is likely to demotivate you, without improving your acting skills or your chances of finding work.

## REAL WORK VS. BUSY WORK

There is a distinction between working hard, and working hard at the right things.

Working hard at the right things means focusing on something that is relevant to your casting ability.

Doing so makes it easier to identify what you need to do to reach your full potential as an actor.

Once you identify areas of improvement that are relevant to your employability, consistency is key.

It is essential to stick to what you are doing, so you can make progress.

In contrast, if your hard work is simply busy work, it will occupy your time without leading to any visible signs of progress.

You will spend your energy on lots of different projects or skills, yet not have a clear strategy or purpose.

By continuously switching focus, nothing has a chance to build and your efforts end up going to waste.

Many actors spend a lot of time being busy without getting anywhere.

They may have a preferred acting technique, and they may equate that with having a way to improve their acting.

However, knowing how to use a specific acting technique will only help you improve if you are disciplined about working on your craft.

What these actors need is a process they can trust, though with they can get better day by day.

## A NEED FOR SELF-EFFICACY

When you don't know whether your actions are making any difference, you lack what psychologists call "self-efficacy"–the confidence that your hard work will bear fruit.

Your level of self-efficacy influences how likely you are to persist when confronting difficulties.

If you have high self-efficacy, you are more likely to attempt difficult tasks and maintain your focus in the face of setbacks.

By contrast, if you have low self-efficacy, you are unlikely to remain consistent with your efforts.

Why persevere if there is no point? Continuously doubting yourself makes it easy to give up.

To have high self-efficacy, you need a process you can trust.

Beyond having a preferred acting technique, you need a clear structure that will make it easier to decide where to devote your time and energy at any one time.

This includes knowing how to set goals that will help you become a better actor, making time for working on your craft, measuring your progress, and reviewing your goals as you improve.

In the next chapter, we will explore the most common way actors sabotage themselves when they lack clarity.

## KEY POINTS

- Most actors lack clarity on how to reach their full potential.
- As they don't know where to focus their efforts, they engage in lots of random acting-related activities that do not result in measurable progress.
- Hard work only leads to progress if it is focused, consistent, and relevant to what would help you become a better actor.
- When you don't know whether your actions are making a difference, you do not have "self-efficacy"–the confidence that your efforts will bear fruit.
- Lacking self-efficacy makes it difficult to stay consistent with your efforts, gradually decreasing your motivation.
- To achieve excellence as an actor, you need a process that leads to measurable progress and is relevant to your employability.

# CHAPTER 2

# THE TALENT FALLACY

## THE PROBLEM WITH TALENT

Actors who struggle with making progress often blame their inability to reach their full potential not on their lack of clarity, but on their lack of talent.

Talent refers to a natural ability that allows you to do something better than others.

A talent is something that comes easily to you and that you are good at from the start.

As this is a natural ability, it shows up early in life, usually during childhood.

The word talent is often used in relation to actors.

We talk about whether an actor is talented, or whether one actor is more talented than another.

We also see talent as an essential ingredient of an actor's success.

But what if you are starting to wonder whether you are talented enough to be an actor?

The problem with the notion of talent is that it is innate. As such, it flies in the face of your self-efficacy.

If you think that talent is crucial to achieving excellence as an actor, and that you lack talent, this is not something you can change, no matter how hard you try.

Not being talented is as if the odds were stacked against you from the start.

Even entertaining the thought that one day you could achieve excellence feels like you are deluding yourself.

What happens, then, when you realize that you have not been getting better at your craft despite trying lots of different things?

At such moments, the most likely outcome is that you will attribute your inability to make progress to your lack of talent, instead of a lack of clarity in what you can do to improve.

As a result, you may lose hope and eventually

give up on your acting dream, instead of persevering and looking for ways to get better.

## TALENT AND HIGH ACHIEVEMENT

Research on high achievers shows that even though talent exists, it is irrelevant when it comes to achieving excellence.

As Geoff Colvin argues in *Talent Is Overrated*, talent is indeed a good predictor of performance, but only if a task is unfamiliar.

For example, if you have a talent for drawing, you can pick up a pencil and create a beautiful picture on your first attempt.

However, once you have been doing something for a while, talent is no longer a good predictor of performance.

Many extraordinary artists were not considered talented when they began working on their craft, yet that initial lack of talent became irrelevant as they kept practicing and their mastery began to emerge.

Achieving excellence takes many years of hard graft; there is no fast track to excellence.

As you put in the hours, talent no longer plays a role in that equation.

Research shows that most so-called "gifted" children do not become high achievers.

Although they may bring something special into the world, their brilliance is short-lived if they do not put in the hard work required to turn that initial talent into mastery.

A reassuring finding, if you do not consider yourself talented, is that many people who achieved greatness in their field did not show evidence of talent during childhood.

Researchers have established the now famous "ten-year rule:" it takes a decade or more to achieve excellence, and some require even longer.

This ten-year rule has been substantiated by research on high achievers in various fields, such as chess, math, science, musical composition, swimming, tennis, and literature.

In all these areas, not even the most "talented" achieved excellence without ten years of hard work.

## THE MULTIPLIER EFFECT

Talent does contribute to high achievement, but only if particular circumstances are present.

For example, let's say that as a child, you were

cast as the lead in a school play and gave a good performance.

You may have delighted in the applause from the audience, and your parents may have been so impressed with your performance that they decided to send you to an age-appropriate drama school as an extracurricular activity.

As a result of this small early advantage, you may have received more drama training than your peers, making it easier to secure an agent and start going to auditions.

This is the so-called "multiplier effect."

However, this effect can only lead to excellence if you are prepared to put in lots of practice over many years. Talent, by itself, does not guarantee high achievement.

In the next chapter, we will explore how believing you are talented can even become an impediment to excellence if accompanied by certain limiting beliefs.

## KEY POINTS

- Actors who struggle with making progress often blame their inability to reach their full potential not on their lack of clarity, but on their lack of talent.

- The notion of talent flies in the face of your self-efficacy.
- If you don't have talent and believe that talent is essential to achieving excellence as an actor, you may conclude there is no point in working hard to improve; it will simply not happen.
- Research shows that even though talent exists, and a person with talent stands out when they attempt an unfamiliar task, talent decreases in importance as the task becomes more familiar and true mastery begins to emerge.
- Talent only provides a small advantage, and only if other favorable circumstances are present.
- By itself, talent does not guarantee high achievement, nor is it an essential ingredient of excellence.

# CHAPTER 3

# TALENT AND THE FIXED MINDSET

## TALENT AS A POTENTIAL OBSTACLE

In the previous chapter, we explored the limiting belief that achieving excellence as an actor is impossible if you do not have talent.

In this chapter, we will explore the opposite problem: believing you are a talented actor, but letting that turn into a disadvantage.

Of course, talent can be helpful in the pursuit of excellence.

However, it can also become a problem if accompanied by the so-called "fixed mindset"–the belief that your abilities are something you are born with and that you cannot improve upon them in any meaningful way.

The term was coined by Carol Dweck, who researched how the beliefs people hold about their abilities influence their approach to encountering obstacles in their path.

## CONSEQUENCES OF THE FIXED MINDSET

If you are under the influence of the "fixed mindset," you believe that having to put effort into getting better as an actor means that you are not talented enough.

At first glance, you may find this strange. Why would anyone believe that putting in effort to improve could be construed as a bad thing?

Yet think how often you have come across the attitude that, "You've either got it or you don't," within the acting industry–a clear illustration of the fixed mindset.

It is worth considering to what extent this belief has influenced you.

The problem with the fixed mindset is that no matter how talented you are, you will eventually encounter somebody more talented than you.

At that moment, the fixed mindset turns into a disadvantage.

As you start questioning your previous self-beliefs, the fixed mindset becomes a source of countless insecurities.

Instead of working hard to improve, you get distracted by comparing yourself to other actors.

Questions such as, "Will I look brilliant or incompetent?" will likely dominate your thoughts, making you self-conscious and insecure.

In addition, these questions don't just affect the way you view your achievements, but also your friendships and other meaningful relationships.

It is difficult to be friends with people if you are constantly comparing yourself to them.

Many actors have a fixed mindset without realizing it, often due to limiting beliefs they picked up from their families or educational environments.

If you are one of these actors, changing your way of thinking will open up a whole new world of possibilities.

## THE GROWTH MINDSET

The fixed mindset stands in stark contrast to what Carol Dweck calls the "growth mindset."

Actors who have a growth mindset believe that their abilities and intelligence can be developed over time through effort and practice, regardless of any talent they are born with.

These actors do not feel the need to prove their superiority over others, nor do they become demotivated when encountering someone who is doing better.

Instead, they are eager to learn from their more successful peers and persist in the face of difficulties.

As a result, actors who have a growth mindset are likely to be more motivated, resilient, and successful than their peers.

## DEVELOPING A GROWTH MINDSET

The great thing about the growth mindset is that it can be learned.

To do so, start reframing any weaknesses in your acting abilities as opportunities for growth.

When you have a growth mindset, you measure success not in relation to others, but in relation to yourself, before and after effort.

Research shows that this tiny mindset shift significantly improves your chances of achieving excellence.

If you primarily see yourself through the lens

of the fixed mindset, experimenting with the growth mindset will allow you to explore a new way of being.

Developing a growth mindset will also feel like a huge relief, as it will reduce the pressure to display perfection and come out on top in every situation.

When you embrace the growth mindset, you only fail when you don't put in the effort to improve.

Effort is seen as a good thing, because it makes you better than you were before.

As long as you keep working on the right things, you will get closer to excellence day by day.

The process of deliberate practice, which we will start exploring in the next chapter, offers you a clear structure for applying the growth mindset to achieving excellence as an actor.

## KEY POINTS

- Talent can become an impediment to high achievement if it is accompanied by the "fixed mindset."

- This mindset rests on the premise that if you are talented at something, you do not have to put in the effort to improve.
- Having a fixed mindset can become a problem for actors, as it prevents them from putting in the effort to achieve excellence.
- In contrast to the fixed mindset stands the "growth mindset."
- Actors with a growth mindset know they must put in effort to improve, regardless of their level of talent.
- As a result, they see mistakes and challenges as an invitation to keep working on their craft instead of problems to be hidden from others.

CHAPTER 4

# DELIBERATE PRACTICE FOR ACTORS

## DEMOCRATIZING HIGH ACHIEVEMENT

To become a better actor, you need a growth mindset–whether or not you consider yourself talented.

This means you must be prepared to put in lots of effort and get out of your comfort zone.

There is a process for applying the growth mindset to acting; it is called "deliberate practice."

Deliberate practice is a specific type of practice that improves performance on a particular skill.

It involves breaking down any skill you want to master into its component parts and identifying the ones that fall outside your comfort zone.

You then practice these parts over and over until you achieve mastery.

## THE DELIBERATE PRACTICE MINDSET

Deliberate practice differs from what most call "practice," which usually consists of mindless repetition.

When using deliberate practice, you focus on one specific aspect of your craft in great detail.

The goal you set is not about a particular outcome, but about the process of reaching that outcome.

For example, let's say you would like to improve your audition technique.

Most actors would set their sights on the outcome, which is to get cast.

However, if you wanted to use deliberate practice to improve your audition technique, that is not the kind of goal you would aim for.

How do you get better at getting cast? There are so many aspects to casting, most of which are not within your control.

Instead, you would set a goal that focuses on the process of auditioning.

For example, you could set the goal of using your breath to stay relaxed while waiting to be invited into the audition room.

You could be even more specific, such as deciding on a ratio of inbreaths to outbreaths, which would give you something to focus on while waiting.

Initially, you could do all your practice sessions at home, where you can control your environment. This would allow you to focus on your breath fully.

Once you master this skill, you could do some of your practice sessions before doing a self-tape, yet still in the comfort of your own home.

Finally, you could start practicing this skill in the "real" world while waiting your turn in an in-person audition.

Even though your deliberate practice goal is not about getting the part, you can see how mastering the art of relaxation by using your breath would help.

Staying relaxed during the often-agonizing waiting period would allow you to perform better during your audition, bringing you closer to getting cast.

As an actor, deliberate practice offers clarity on how to reach your full potential.

This type of practice allows you to identify areas of improvement in your craft and gives you a structure for making noticeable progress.

Using deliberate practice, you can turn your weaknesses into strengths.

Most importantly, deliberate practice democratizes high achievement by giving you a way out of any limiting beliefs regarding your level of talent.

Using deliberate practice, you can improve at anything, regardless of your innate abilities, as long as you focus your energy and time correctly.

The benefits of deliberate practice have been demonstrated by many high achievers across different disciplines, including athletes, musicians, and chess masters.

As such, when you use deliberate practice, you can benefit from a high level of self-efficacy, because this kind of practice has a proven track record of success.

Deliberate practice has yet to be publicly embraced by actors, but this is where your opportunity lies.

Using deliberate practice allows you to differentiate yourself within a competitive industry.

Throughout the rest of the book, we will explore how to apply deliberate practice to the acting craft.

To do so, we first need to identify the steps involved in deliberate practice, which we will discuss in the next chapter.

## KEY POINTS

- Deliberate practice democratizes high achievement by offering clarity on how to reach your full potential.
- When doing deliberate practice, you focus on a specific skill you would like to master, break it down into its component parts, and work on the ones that fall outside your comfort zone until you achieve mastery.
- The goal you set is not about the outcome, but about the process of reaching that outcome.
- High achievers across various disciplines, including athletics, music,

and chess, have demonstrated the
benefits of deliberate practice.

# CHAPTER 5

# THE PROCESS OF DELIBERATE PRACTICE

## A TEMPLATE FOR DELIBERATE PRACTICE

There are several distinct steps in the process of deliberate practice:

- Setting a practice goal
- Doing the practice
- Evaluating the practice
- Setting a new practice goal

In this chapter, we will discuss each of these steps and explore how to apply them to the acting craft.

## SETTING A PRACTICE GOAL

The first (and often the most difficult) step when doing deliberate practice is to decide on the goal you will work on during your next series of practice sessions.

As mentioned in the previous chapter, when you use deliberate practice, you set goals that are not about the outcome, but about the process of reaching that outcome.

This goal should be tailored to you and what you want to improve at that particular moment.

Part of this process is learning to identify where your so-called "learning zone" lies.

Your learning zone is the place between what you are already comfortable doing (your "comfort zone") and what is beyond your current level of skill (your "panic zone").

The better you get at identifying your learning zone, the easier it is to choose a deliberate practice goal that leads to quick and noticeable progress.

Your other task, at this stage of the process, is to set a standard by which to evaluate how you did once the practice is over.

## DOING THE PRACTICE

The second stage of the process is self-explanatory–doing the practice.

Depending on the task you have chosen as your goal, you may be able to observe yourself as you are doing the practice.

This means you step outside yourself, monitor what is happening in your mind, and ask how your practice is going.

This is similar to meditation; you watch your thoughts as they come and go.

## EVALUATING THE PRACTICE

Once the practice session is over, you evaluate how you did against the standard you decided on while setting the practice goal.

This evaluation must be detailed, so you can measure your progress and identify areas of improvement.

In undertaking this evaluation, you must embrace a non-judgmental attitude.

The purpose of this evaluation is to understand how you did and what you could improve in the future, not to make yourself feel bad.

## SETTING A NEW PRACTICE GOAL

If you find things you could improve in the future during the evaluation stage, take note.

Use what you learned to set a more specific goal for the next practice session.

Through using deliberate practice, your learning zone will shift.

What was once your learning zone will become your comfort zone, and what was once your panic zone will become your new learning zone.

Evaluating your practice helps you recognize when it is time to adjust your goals.

This means you keep your learning zone moving, instead of reaching a plateau and no longer making progress.

## APPLYING DELIBERATE PRACTICE TO ACTING

How do you apply these stages of deliberate practice to the acting craft?

Although deliberate practice has been shown to work in a wide variety of disciplines, there are important differences to consider.

Acting is not like tennis, where you can master

certain difficult shots and improve your chances of success.

With acting, there are many other aspects to take into account.

This makes the first task–identifying a practice goal–more difficult than in other fields.

In the next chapter, we will explore how to choose a goal for your deliberate practice sessions.

## KEY POINTS

- Deliberate practice entails several distinct stages: setting a practice goal, doing the practice, evaluating how you did, and setting a new practice goal.
- The first stage is to set a goal and decide how to measure progress.
- In setting a goal, you need to identify your "learning zone," which is more challenging than your "comfort zone," yet not as overwhelming as your "panic zone."
- The second stage is to do the practice, and–if you can–observe yourself doing it.

- The third stage is to evaluate how you did during the practice, based on the standard you decided on during the first stage.
- The fourth stage is to use what you learned during the evaluation stage to set a new goal.
- As you gain mastery, you must adjust your goal to keep yourself in the "learning zone" and continue to develop your skill level.

# CHAPTER 6

## CHOOSING YOUR PRACTICE GOAL

### EXPLORING GENERAL AREAS OF IMPROVEMENT

In this chapter, we will discuss how to set a goal that will help you improve as an actor.

As the first step in this process, let us consider the range of acting-related areas where you could use deliberate practice:

- Improve your camera auditions
- Work on a monologue
- Run your lines
- Networking, especially remembering names, how to introduce yourself, etc.

- Telling stories about yourself, e.g., in interviews
- Specific skills that could get you work (e.g., learning a musical instrument)
- Get better at using a specific acting technique
- Mastering a particular accent
- Working on your voice and diction
- Mastering a specific singing style

These are only a few suggestions to help you start thinking of the many ways you could use deliberate practice.

Add any other areas of improvement that are relevant to you.

Once you are done, you may feel that the list of things you could be getting better at as an actor is endless–and perhaps overwhelming.

However, there is one thing that will allow you to narrow down your focus: casting.

## CASTING CONSIDERATIONS

As an actor, you are constrained by your physicality.

This means there are certain roles for which

you will not be considered because of how you look and the general energy you bring.

Although frustrating, this constraint can help you narrow down your focus.

To use casting as a guide when choosing your deliberate practice goals, consider the kinds of stories you can tell through your physical presence.

In doing so, keep an eye on the list of skills or other improvements you had considered earlier.

Ask yourself what would get you the most work, given your specific casting potential.

For example, do you have the kind of look that would lend itself well to Westerns?

In that case, it may be worthwhile to learn skills such as horse riding.

Or perhaps you are easy to cast in period features, in which case you may need to master the kinds of accents that would help you do better in those auditions.

By being clear on your casting potential, you can identify the skills that, once mastered, will get you more work.

The point of striving for excellence is to make yourself more employable as an actor.

The more work you can get, the more you will

practice your craft, and the more your overall level of mastery will improve.

## FURTHER REFINING YOUR GOAL

By now, you hopefully have a better idea of the specific skill or aspect of your craft you would like to work on in your first set of deliberate practice sessions.

If so, it is time to go one step further in refining your goal.

As mentioned in a previous chapter, the goal you set for deliberate practice is not about the overall outcome you want to achieve–e.g., getting cast–but about the process of achieving that outcome.

This means that once you decide on a specific skill or aspect of your craft you want to work on, you need to break that down further into its individual components.

Take some time now to identify these.

In addition, reflect on which of these feels the most challenging to you; that is the one you need to focus on first.

## FOCUS LEADS TO EXCELLENCE

If you approach the overall goal of achieving excellence as an actor in this strategic way, it becomes less abstract and more achievable.

To be a great actor, you don't have to become exceptional at all aspects of acting, including voice work, accents, combat skills, presence, and so on.

You need to identify a few elements of your craft that are particularly relevant to the roles you are likely to get cast in and use deliberate practice to become exceptional at those.

The better you understand the kinds of stories you can tell through your physical presence, the easier it becomes to identify gaps in your existing skills and set your deliberate practice goals.

In the next chapter, we will address several factors worth keeping in mind when choosing a deliberate practice goal.

## KEY POINTS

- Acting does not have an easily definable set of skills, so choosing the right goal to focus on can be more complicated than in other fields.

- To narrow down the list of options, consider your casting potential and ask yourself what you could improve to make yourself more employable.
- Once you decide on one specific aspect of your craft you want to work on, break that down into its individual components.
- By narrowing down your focus, you will likely find that achieving excellence is more attainable than you had thought.

# CHAPTER 7

# GOAL-SETTING FOR DELIBERATE PRACTICE

## MAKING GOAL-SETTING EASIER

For actors, setting a goal is the most challenging aspect of deliberate practice.

In the previous chapter, we discussed how to narrow down the list of options to make the process easier.

However, focusing on the specific aspect you will choose is only part of setting a deliberate practice goal.

To maximize your chances of success, several factors are worth considering, as we will discuss in this chapter.

## ONE GOAL AT A TIME

When first starting to use deliberate practice, it is tempting to want to work on different aspects of your craft in parallel.

For example, you may want to spend some of your deliberate practice sessions working on a difficult accent, and others on improving your audition technique–all on the same day.

In the beginning, when deliberate practice is still new and exciting, this may be feasible.

You may enjoy a few exhilarating days using deliberate practice to blitz through several challenging skills and delight in watching yourself gain mastery at dizzying speed.

As motivating as this may be initially, maintaining this rhythm is not sustainable long-term.

Because of the level of focus you need, using deliberate practice places a huge strain on your cognitive resources.

As such, if you put too much pressure on yourself and expect to maintain the same speed of progress over time, you will soon burn out and lose your motivation.

If you are serious about using deliberate practice to achieve excellence as an actor, it is best if you only work on one goal at a time, and stick to that goal until you have reached the standard you set.

Then–and only then–pick a different goal to work on.

By preventing burnout, focusing on one goal will allow you to make faster progress than if you were working on multiple goals.

In addition, concentrating on one aspect of your craft will allow you to become more creative and resourceful in how you go about improving that one aspect.

Our minds get slowed down by having too many areas to focus on.

By only working on one deliberate practice goal at a time, you are giving that goal maximum processing power, which makes progress inevitable.

If you are skeptical, approach this as an experiment.

Try focusing on only one goal in your deliberate practice sessions for at least one week.

You will see the difference this will make to the speed with which you can make progress.

## PRIORITIZE CLARITY OVER ACTION

The point of setting a deliberate practice goal is to gain clarity over what to do, instead of engaging in aimless activity.

Using deliberate practice is as much about what you are *not* going to do as it is about what you *are* going to do.

If you are still unsure what you aim to achieve with your sessions or how you will evaluate your progress, spend more time on planning.

Your plan should include a specific goal you will pursue during your sessions and what actions you will undertake to reach that goal.

The more clarity you have, the more motivated you will be.

Having clarity also helps your sense of self-efficacy–trusting that your actions will make a difference.

## TRACKING YOUR PROGRESS

Before starting to work on a goal, consider how you will evaluate and track your progress.

How will you decide when you have mastered something?

For example, if you are working on an accent, what counts as having mastered that accent?

You may decide your goal will be met once someone thinks you are from that part of the world, or once you get cast after using that accent in an audition.

There is no right or wrong answer, but it is important to decide on this standard before starting your deliberate practice sessions, so you know what you are aiming for.

You must also decide how to track your progress and identify the milestones you plan to reach.

The more clarity you have on the specific actions you need to take, the quicker you will make progress on your goal.

In the next chapter, we will turn our attention to the things you must keep in mind while doing deliberate practice.

## KEY POINTS

- Only work on one goal at a time. This will allow you to make faster progress and remain consistent with your commitment to deliberate practice.

- Prioritize clarity over action. If you are unsure what you aim to achieve with your sessions and what you are going to do to reach your goal, spend more time on planning.
- Decide in advance how to evaluate your progress, what your milestones will be, and what counts as having completed a specific goal.

# CHAPTER 8

# DOING THE PRACTICE

## THE DELIBERATE PRACTICE MINDSET

You probably have a clearer idea by now of a particular skill or aspect of your craft you would like to work on using deliberate practice.

In this chapter, we will discuss how to approach your practice sessions.

By necessity, this guidance is somewhat vague, as the specifics of what your practice sessions look like will vary depending on the goal you set.

However, there are general principles that apply to deliberate practice across the board; that is what we will focus on.

## MINDFULNESS DURING REPETITION

One crucial aspect of doing deliberate practice, regardless of your goal, is the intention to keep your mind focused on the task.

Repeating something over and over makes it easy to slip into automatic mode; this will not lead to progress.

Doing deliberate practice means fully engaging with your goal instead of letting your mind wander.

By avoiding automatic behavior, you are giving yourself the opportunity to adapt what you do and to learn with every new iteration.

Staying focused on the goal, despite countless repetitions, is a skill that takes time to learn.

Once you do, it will improve your ability to get better at whatever you decide.

To maintain this high level of focus, keep your initial practice sessions short–perhaps around ten minutes, and no longer than half an hour.

In addition, give yourself plenty of rest between practice sessions, to allow your brain to recover from the mental focus that deliberate practice requires.

## DEVELOPING SENSITIVITY TO NUANCE

Another important aspect of every practice session is developing sensitivity to nuance.

This means that you should start noticing how each iteration differs from the one before, to figure out how to get closer to the standard you set.

For example, let's say you are using deliberate practice to work on a particular accent and are focusing on a specific sound.

How is every time you use that sound different from the previous time?

What changes are you making with each repetition to bring yourself closer to the standard you need to achieve?

It is this sensitivity to nuance that allows you to improve with every step.

Eventually, as you maintain this level of attention to detail, you will perceive more than most people would.

As a result, you will become more intentional in what you focus on and speed up your progress.

To an outsider, what you are doing may look boring, because of the repetitive nature of deliberate practice.

In fact, you are cultivating a fascination with

the nuances that make each attempt different from the others.

Over time, these tiny differences lead to mastery.

## PURSUING A FLOW STATE

When things go well, you will achieve what Mihaly Csikszentmihalyi calls "a flow state."

This state of pure focus creates a perfect balance between being calm and being alert to the task at hand.

You cannot make this flow state happen at will, but you can set up the circumstances where achieving this state is possible.

When you are in a flow state, you can observe yourself doing the practice and make adjustments as needed.

To keep making progress, it is also essential that you devote time to evaluating the practice session once it is over.

In the next chapter, we will discuss this evaluation process in more depth.

## KEY POINTS

- Using deliberate practice means focusing on what you are doing, instead of allowing your mind to slip into automatic mode.
- Through maintaining focus, you can adapt what you do and learn with every iteration.
- Being mindful also helps you develop your sensitivity to nuance.
- Eventually, you will perceive more than most people would, which means you become more detailed and intentional in what you focus on during your practice sessions.
- By keeping these principles in mind, you are creating the ideal circumstances to experience a flow state while doing deliberate practice.

# CHAPTER 9

# EVALUATING THE PRACTICE

## THE IMPORTANCE OF EVALUATING YOUR PRACTICE

Once the practice session is over, you must evaluate how you did.

This evaluation will inform the goal you set for your next deliberate practice session.

In addition, evaluating how you did allows you to acknowledge your progress and keeps you motivated to keep going.

In this chapter, we will explore three ways to complete this part of the process: self-evaluating, evaluating your progress using a camera, and asking for another person's feedback.

## SELF-EVALUATING AFTER THE PRACTICE

The easiest way to evaluate your practice is to reflect on how it went immediately after the session.

I advise that you do a short self-evaluation after every session to help you decide on your next steps.

In addition, aim to do an in-depth weekly or monthly self-evaluation to review your overall progress.

It is best to write down your self-reflections in a notebook and to have a process in place for what you will focus on.

This will allow you to see yourself making progress over time and identify areas you need to address.

Make sure not to undermine your self-confidence when going through this self-evaluation process.

As we discussed in chapter 5, deliberate practice pushes you out of your comfort zone and into your learning zone.

This means that it forces you to stretch yourself beyond your current strengths and explore some of your weaknesses.

The problem is that going outside your comfort

zone can trigger your so-called "inner critic," a term that refers to negative self-talk that is judgmental and unkind.

The inner critic will likely bring out your perfectionism, which will make it harder to step outside your comfort zone.

How can you distinguish between the helpful evaluation that deliberate practice requires and inner critic interference?

When entering the evaluation stage of deliberate practice, you need a growth mindset, which we discussed in chapter 3.

Approach any mistakes as learning opportunities instead of reasons to feel bad about yourself.

Become curious about your mistakes and everything they can teach you about improving your process.

When approaching the evaluation stage with a growth mindset, your criticism is different in intention and tone from when you allow your inner critic to take charge.

The growth mindset directs your attention towards what you are currently doing and what you could be doing differently.

This non-judgmental evaluation motivates you

to look for ways to improve; it does not demotivate you by making you feel bad about yourself.

By evaluating how you did using the growth mindset, you can adjust your practice and devise further deliberate practice sessions where you focus in more detail on what needs to change.

## USING A CAMERA FOR YOUR EVALUATION

You may also want to use a camera (or an audio recording device, where relevant) to record your deliberate practice sessions and watch the recording to see how you did.

Watching a recording of yourself gives you a level of objectivity that is difficult to achieve through self-reflection.

Using a camera may be particularly useful if you work primarily in film or TV, although recording yourself can also help with certain aspects of stage work.

Here are a few ideas on types of deliberate practice where using a camera might be especially useful:

- Record a monologue–or maybe even parts of a monologue. Work on a particular intention you want to convey. What is the character trying to do with their words?

- Record yourself speaking in a particular accent. This makes it easier to identify areas of improvement and keep practicing those until you get them right.
- Read a new script in front of a mock "casting team" panel–maybe a few of your friends. Watching a recording of this session will help you identify what you need to improve in the way you split your attention. Mastering this skill will allow you to make a great first impression when you are given a script just before an audition.
- Filming yourself can help you evaluate specific elements of your performance. Does your acting look natural and believable? What are you doing with your face? Are you conveying what you are hoping to convey?
- Record yourself playing an instrument and keep practicing until you get it right.

- Record yourself singing a song and evaluate how well you are connecting with the lyrics.
- Work on choreography.

## ASKING OTHERS FOR FEEDBACK

Other people's feedback is valuable because they can see what you are doing in a way you cannot see yourself.

Receiving feedback from others may be something you do regularly, or something you do after a period of working on a skill by yourself.

However, be careful whom you ask for feedback at this early stage.

On the one hand, you want someone who can give you honest feedback and suggest ways to improve.

On the other hand, you will be showing them a skill you are still developing.

As such, it is important that the person providing the feedback understands this and does not demotivate you by being too harsh.

Finding someone who can strike this balance may take some time, and you may need to try out several people before you find the right person.

In the next chapter, we will explore the process of using what you learned during your evaluation to set a new deliberate practice goal.

## KEY POINTS

- To make progress, you need to get into the habit of evaluating your practice. You can do so through self-reflection, using a camera, and asking others for feedback.
- When self-evaluating, record your reflections in a journal, so you can look back over your progress as your practice develops. Evaluate yourself in a way that is constructive and motivating as opposed to demoralizing.
- Using a camera allows you to go beyond biased self-reflection and gain some objectivity over what you are doing during your practice.
- If you ask someone else for feedback, make sure you choose the right person, someone who can help you grow without damaging your self-confidence.

# CHAPTER 10

# SETTING A NEW GOAL

## REGULARLY REVISING YOUR GOAL

Deliberate practice comes with a lot of goal-setting at various stages of the process.

We have already discussed how the end of every practice session provides an opportunity for setting a new goal.

This goal will be based on how the session went and what you need to change to make further progress.

However, to ensure that you are making meaningful progress, you must also periodically review how you are doing by examining your overall level of improvement.

Those times present the opportunity to set a

different kind of new goal–one that relates to the big picture of your quest for excellence.

As a result of this evaluation, you may decide that you have mastered the skill you were working on and want to focus your next set of deliberate practice sessions on a completely different skill or aspect of your craft.

Alternatively, you may decide to keep working on the same skill, but set a more ambitious target that reflects your improved abilities.

This new target may be something that was completely outside the realm of possibility a while back, but is becoming more attainable given your most recent progress.

Whether you are taking on a completely different skill or setting a new target, pursuing this new big-picture goal will take you outside your newly established comfort zone.

Stepping outside your comfort zone in this way, and doing so on a regular basis, is not easy.

However, it is necessary if you are serious about aiming for excellence.

## STEPPING OUTSIDE YOUR COMFORT ZONE

Stepping outside your comfort zone is likely to feel counter-intuitive at first.

Why not play to your strengths and keep doing what you are already good at without challenging yourself?

The problem is that if you stay within your comfort zone, you are not allowing yourself to grow as an actor.

Deliberate practice is about continuously stretching yourself.

If you are serious about using deliberate practice to achieve excellence, you must keep stretching yourself beyond your comfort zone and into your new learning zone.

## THE LEARNING ZONE KEEPS SHIFTING

By using deliberate practice on a specific element of your craft, your learning zone will shift.

What was once your learning zone will become your comfort zone, and what was once your panic zone will become your learning zone.

As such, your goal needs to shift too, so you keep yourself in the learning zone.

Part of learning to use deliberate practice long-term is becoming good at identifying when you need to set a new goal and where your new learning zone lies.

Engaging in this process of constantly re-evaluating your goals and pushing yourself out of your comfort zone requires a lot of motivation.

In the next chapter, we will discuss how to motivate yourself, so you can remain consistent in using deliberate practice.

## KEY POINTS

- As you start using deliberate practice regularly, you will soon gain mastery over an element of your craft that was outside your comfort zone.
- At that point, it becomes tempting to stick to this new comfort zone. However, deliberate practice is about continuously stretching yourself.
- Regularly review your practice goal and be prepared to adjust it to match your increasing level of mastery.
- As you improve, keep pushing your target slightly outside your comfort

zone, so you keep yourself within your new learning zone and continue to grow.

- Alternatively, you may use this period of re-evaluation to acknowledge your new mastery over a particular skill and decide to focus your next set of deliberate practice sessions on mastering a new skill.

# CHAPTER 11

# FINDING MOTIVATION

## FACING THE MOTIVATION DIP

When you start using deliberate practice, you will likely experience an initial "honeymoon phase."

During this time, you will be excited to try out this new process and delight at how quickly you are improving.

However, sooner or later, this honeymoon phase will come to an end.

Instead, you will find yourself in what Seth Godin calls "the dip"–the stretch of time in the middle of a long journey when a project is no longer novel or exciting and you start questioning whether to keep going.

In this chapter, we will explore how to motivate yourself long-term, beyond the honeymoon phase.

## BRAIN CHEMISTRY AND MOTIVATION

Many believe motivation is similar to a character trait; you either have it or you don't.

In fact, research on motivation shows that given the right circumstances, motivation grows.

As such, if you know how to set things up the right way, you can *become* motivated to do something–such as using deliberate practice to improve your craft.

One of the biggest influences on your level of motivation is your brain chemistry.

Depending on your brain chemistry, your motivation can go up or down.

In our day-to-day lives, our brain chemistry changes without our conscious intent, leading to either an increase or a decrease in our level of motivation.

However, you can learn to consciously work with your brain chemistry to maximize your motivation.

By learning to change your brain chemistry, you can gain control over your motivation, making it possible to remain consistent in using deliberate practice once the novelty wears off.

## DOPAMINE AS A MOTIVATION BOOSTER

The easiest and most sustainable way to use your brain chemistry as a motivation booster is to encourage your brain to release dopamine, a so-called "happy chemical."

Your brain releases dopamine when you set a goal and start pursuing it.

In fact, the mere act of setting a goal encourages your brain to release dopamine.

Our brain craves goals–they are the modern equivalent of the food sources our ancestors were continuously looking for in their environment.

When you set a goal, your evolution-influenced brain thinks, "There's a juicy reward–let's go after it!" and releases a burst of dopamine to give you the energy you need.

When you set lots of small and achievable goals, you gain access to lots of small bursts of dopamine; these are pleasurable and motivating.

For this reason, the best way to motivate yourself when dealing with a task you must do over and over, as is the case with deliberate practice, is to game-ify your progress.

## GAME-IFYING YOUR PROGRESS

By using game-ification during your deliberate practice sessions, you are giving yourself lots of small goals to reach, thus encouraging your brain to keep releasing dopamine.

Game-ifying your progress is easy when doing deliberate practice.

Set a goal for your practice sessions and once you reach it consistently, set a slightly higher goal going forward.

This goal can be related to anything you like, such as the number of iterations during your practice session or a specific target for each iteration.

For example, let's say you are learning to juggle.

The goal you set could be about any number of things: how long each practice session will last, how many balls you will juggle with, how long you can keep juggling before dropping a ball, and so on.

To maximize your motivation, make your initial goal easily achievable.

By giving yourself an easy win, you are eliminating any resistance to taking this initial step.

In addition, set your subsequent goal only minimally higher than the previous one.

Doing so consistently will allow you to reach your new targets quickly and get more frequent bursts of dopamine.

If you are interested in an in-depth exploration of how to motivate yourself as an actor, read my book *Motivation for Actors*.

In the next chapter, we will discuss five common barriers to motivation and solutions for overcoming them.

## KEY POINTS

- One of the greatest difficulties with deliberate practice is keeping yourself motivated for the long haul, once the "honeymoon phase" of doing something new is over.
- To motivate yourself long-term, you must learn to harness the so-called "happy chemical" dopamine.
- The easiest way to encourage your brain to release dopamine when doing

something as repetitive as deliberate practice is to game-ify your progress.

- Set an easily achievable goal for your practice. Once you reach it consistently, set a slightly higher goal going forward.

# CHAPTER 12

# OVERCOMING BARRIERS TO MOTIVATION

## THE CHALLENGE OF MAINTAINING CONSISTENCY

In the previous chapter, we discussed how to motivate yourself to keep using deliberate practice throughout your acting career, instead of giving up as soon as the "honeymoon phase" is over.

In this chapter, we will explore five motivation barriers that might come up as you start using deliberate practice on a regular basis.

The insights relating to these barriers originate from the Buddhist tradition, where they are called the "five hindrances."

In that tradition, the five hindrances are taught

as a way to maintain a consistent meditation practice.

Each of these hindrances has a so-called "antidote" that helps in overcoming it.

There are many similarities between deliberate practice and meditation, so these old Buddhist insights are worth exploring.

I have adapted these insights, including the antidotes, to the barriers that will likely come up as you start using deliberate practice as an actor.

## FIVE BARRIERS TO MOTIVATION

While reading about the five barriers, see if you can identify the ones that are the most relevant to you.

Then consider how you might overcome these barriers given your particular circumstances.

### *Wanting things to be different*

The first barrier that may come up is about wanting the circumstances to be different.

You may want to have more time to focus on doing deliberate practice, or more money to invest in your acting career.

The problem with this barrier is that it turns

your attention towards something you cannot control, which feels disempowering and decreases your motivation.

The easiest way to overcome this barrier is to shift your focus to the things you can do, given your specific circumstances.

What aspects relating to deliberate practice are within your control?

Focus exclusively on these aspects and stop worrying about anything else.

*Impatience*

Another barrier you may experience is impatience with the speed of progress.

You may feel that you are not making enough progress, that you were doing better before, or that you have hit a roadblock and don't know how to move forward.

Impatience is natural, especially in our fast-paced world.

We are surrounded by things happening at dizzying speed. This influences our brain waves, which match the pace of our environment.

When you come up against this barrier, you must find ways to restore a sense of calm.

Focus on your body, as your body and mind are linked.

You could slow down your breath or pay attention to your heartbeats.

Alternatively, you could focus on your feelings, watching each of them intensify and release, making way for another feeling to arise.

Once you have slowed down your body, shift your attention to acknowledging the progress you have already made.

Consider the milestones you have reached and how far you have come.

When doing deliberate practice every day, gradually improving your skill, it is easy to forget where you started.

Take your time to acknowledge your progress.

At this point in your journey, you need to strengthen your trust in the process.

Eventually, the motivation to keep going will build and this barrier will dissolve.

*Feeling tired*

The third barrier you may come up against is feeling too tired to do deliberate practice.

This barrier can be a tricky one, because sometimes you may indeed run low on energy.

Doing deliberate practice can be mentally exhausting because of the high level of focus it requires.

Especially in the beginning, as you are getting used to it, you may feel more tired than usual.

If so, you need to spend more time resting between sessions instead of pushing yourself beyond your limits.

Alternatively, could your tiredness be caused by overwhelm?

This may be the case if you have set a goal that is too ambitious.

Your body may be trying to escape the overwhelm caused by your overly ambitious goal.

To explore this possibility, set a less ambitious goal for the next few days.

You may find that when you do, you no longer feel tired at the thought of doing deliberate practice.

*Boredom*

Boredom is the most common barrier to continuing with deliberate practice long-term.

This barrier will likely arise as soon as the novelty has worn off and you are out of the "honeymoon phase."

When this barrier comes up, turn your attention to your brain chemistry, as we discussed in the previous chapter.

Game-ify your progress by setting an easy target. Once you reach it consistently, aim slightly higher.

In doing so, you are giving yourself lots of tiny goals to reach, thus encouraging your brain to release dopamine–a great way to overcome boredom and replenish your motivation.

*Doubt*

The fifth barrier is doubt, which often shows up as "shiny new idea syndrome."

This refers to shifting your focus towards a new goal when facing difficulties pursuing your current goal.

You experience shiny new idea syndrome when you abandon your current deliberate practice goal in favor of a new one and keep doing this repeatedly.

This barrier often compounds other barriers, such as impatience or boredom.

It happens because setting a new goal stimulates dopamine, which can become addictive.

You could switch goals for months or years, jumping from one goal to the next, without achieving mastery over any of the skills you work on.

If you consistently get distracted, you are likely to lose confidence in your ability to get anything done.

As a result, you will get less motivated with every goal you set, because deep down, you will doubt whether you can achieve it.

Get into the habit of recognizing when you are in danger of being lured away from your current goal by shiny new idea syndrome.

The more skilled you become at recognizing what is going on, the less you will give in to temptation.

## NURTURING YOUR CURIOSITY

Once you identify which barriers are the most relevant to you, experiment with different ways of overcoming them.

Be curious about what works for you in overcoming these barriers.

Approaching this as an experiment will transform these barriers into opportunities for learning and growth.

In the next chapter, we will delve deeper into one particular barrier that might come up, and how to overcome it: not having enough time to do deliberate practice.

## KEY POINTS

- After the "honeymoon phase" is over, there are five barriers to motivation that you need to be aware of and counteract, so you can keep using deliberate practice long-term.
- If you get distracted by wanting your circumstances to be different, shift your focus to the things you can control and let go of everything else.
- If you are impatient with your progress, shift your focus to your body by slowing your breath. This will slow down your mind and reduce your impatience.

- If you regularly find yourself too tired to do deliberate practice, you may need more rest between practice sessions. Alternatively, you may need to set a less ambitious goal to reduce the overwhelm that may have caused the tiredness.
- If you get bored with doing deliberate practice, remember to game-ify your progress. By giving yourself lots of small goals to reach, you are encouraging your brain to release dopamine, which will alleviate the boredom.
- If you want to switch to a different deliberate practice goal, you may be suffering from "shiny new idea syndrome." Recognizing this will help you regain your focus.

# CHAPTER 13

# MAKING TIME FOR DELIBERATE PRACTICE

## THE BUSY ACTOR'S LIFE

Doing deliberate practice requires making time for it while juggling bill-paying jobs and other commitments.

If you are like most actors, you may feel there is never enough time in your day to get everything done.

When you have to deal with so many things, how can you add deliberate practice into your day and make it sustainable long-term?

In this chapter, we will explore how to make space in your busy schedule, so you can integrate deliberate practice into your life.

## SETTING A TIME GOAL

The easiest way to ensure you make space for deliberate practice in your daily schedule is to set a time goal.

This simple yet powerful tool will give you the flexibility to fit deliberate practice into your day despite your other commitments.

It will also allow you to relax and recharge once you complete your time goal.

The mechanics of setting a time goal are deceptively simple: decide on the amount of time you will spend on deliberate practice every day and use a timer to ensure you complete that goal before the day is over.

You could set the timer for one hour or half an hour–however long you are confident you can spend on deliberate practice every day.

The length of time is less important than your ability to fulfill your time goal by the end of your day.

Every time you use deliberate practice, let the timer run and make sure to complete your goal before the end of the day.

Whatever length of time you choose, keep it consistent every day, as much as possible.

Consistency is more important than the amount of time you set as your goal.

Even doing twenty minutes of deliberate practice every day will be more beneficial than doing a long session once in a while.

However, stay flexible and adjust your time goal when needed.

For example, if you have an important deadline at your bill-paying job on a particular day, you may only have ten minutes available to dedicate to deliberate practice.

If so, decide in advance that you will lower your time goal for that day.

It is also a good idea to decide in advance that you will not do deliberate practice on a particular day, if you already know you do not have enough time.

Otherwise, if you say to yourself that you will do deliberate practice for a certain amount of time and you don't, your mind will see it as a failure.

This will make it more difficult to motivate yourself the following day.

If you don't reach your goal one day, don't try to make up for the lost time the following day. Reset your timer at the end of each day, ready for the next day.

It is fine if life gets in the way and you don't complete your goal, as long as this does not become a regular thing.

If it does, your time goal may be too ambitious and you need to lower it.

Once the time is up, it is best to stop for the day, even if you have more time available.

Use that time to relax and recharge–you worked hard and deserve a rest.

## USE TIME SPRINTS TO ADD FLEXIBILITY

Whatever your time goal, you will not have to complete all of it in one session.

In fact, it is best if you divide this time into shorter sessions throughout your day by using so-called "sprints."

If, for example, your time goal is to do an hour of deliberate practice a day, you can divide that into three twenty-minute sprints, which you can fit in at various points between your other commitments.

Experiment to see what length of time suits you best for your sprints.

I recommend starting with a five-minute sprint

to warm up, then increasing the sprint length to ten or twenty minutes each.

In the next chapter, we will discuss other factors you may need to consider to integrate deliberate practice into your life.

## KEY POINTS

- Decide how long you will spend doing deliberate practice every day and set a timer at the start of each day to track the time.
- Be realistic with your time goal for deliberate practice and prioritize consistency over ambition.
- Be strict about stopping once the time is up, even if you want to keep going.
- You can split your time goal into shorter sprints of no more than twenty minutes.
- Using sprints will allow your brain to rest and give you greater flexibility to fit deliberate practice among your other commitments.

# CHAPTER 14

# OTHER LIFESTYLE CONSIDERATIONS

## MAKING SPACE FOR DELIBERATE PRACTICE

Committing to deliberate practice long-term is not easy, even if you can see the benefits of taking this step.

If you are thinking of using deliberate practice to achieve excellence as an actor, it is important to understand the magnitude of the commitment you are about to undertake.

Using deliberate practice requires you to arrange your life in particular ways.

There is no existing research on best practices for actors using deliberate practice.

However, there is evidence from high achievers

in other fields about the kinds of lifestyle changes that might be needed.

It is worth reflecting on these factors at this early stage, to create circumstances that will make it easier to remain consistent with using deliberate practice.

## INTEGRATING DELIBERATE PRACTICE INTO YOUR LIFE

The following factors are worth keeping in mind as you embark on this journey.

Use this list as a starting point for considering the specific factors that may be relevant to you.

### *Time requirements*

A consistent finding is that the usual time commitment for deliberate practice is around four hours a day–a considerable requirement.

However, if four hours is impossible given your current circumstances, take heart; it may not be needed.

While this kind of time commitment may be necessary for things like tennis or playing the violin, you may not require this many hours of practice as an actor, at least not on a regular basis.

Unlike a tennis player, you do not need to practice one particular shot repeatedly, or strengthen a specific set of muscles.

One hour a day, perhaps split into three twenty-minute practice sessions, may be enough to practice most of the skills that are relevant to you.

Even so, as you are probably juggling bill-paying jobs and going to auditions, one hour devoted to your craft may still be difficult to achieve.

In that case, remember that deliberate practice is primarily about quality rather than quantity.

If you can keep it consistent, even half an hour a day, split into shorter sprints, may be sufficient.

Think how much progress you could make if you spent half an hour every day working on elements of your craft using deliberate practice.

If this sounds appealing, try using deliberate practice over the course of a week for half an hour a day.

Once you start seeing some improvement, you will likely be motivated to make the necessary changes to integrate deliberate practice into your day.

*Sleep requirements*

Because of the high level of mental alertness you need to do deliberate practice, you may need more sleep than at present.

Several studies have shown that those who use deliberate practice require more sleep, especially naps during the day, in-between practice sessions.

For example, research on violinists showed that violinists who used deliberate practice slept more, not only at night, but also took more afternoon naps.

This is worth knowing, especially when starting out. Do not be surprised if you find yourself more tired than usual.

If this becomes a problem, you may need to schedule some dedicated nap time into your day.

Alternatively, you can fulfill the sleep requirement by scheduling your deliberate practice sessions when you are well-rested.

For example, a study of high-achieving violinists found that they did most of their practice in the late morning or early afternoon, when they were still fresh.

By contrast, low-achieving violinists practiced in the late afternoon, when they were more likely to be tired.

*Financial considerations*

One factor that will make a big difference in maintaining consistency in your practice is your bill-paying job.

Assuming you are not yet at a stage in your acting career where you can make a full-time living from your acting, you probably have one or more bill-paying jobs.

To do deliberate practice long-term, it is essential to find bill-paying work that does not get in the way of your daily commitment to deliberate practice.

If your current job does not allow you to integrate deliberate practice into your day, you may need to consider alternatives.

Perhaps you require a lower-paying job that allows you more flexibility in how you structure your day, or that will enable you to dedicate your most "awake" time to deliberate practice.

You could also find ways of earning a living that involve passive income.

Although setting up passive income streams takes time, it may be worth it in the long run.

You could set up a few side hustles that allow you to pay your bills, so that you can dedicate the most significant portion of your day to your acting career.

Deliberate practice offers you a process that leads to measurable improvement; you know this is a good investment of your time and energy.

This sense of self-efficacy will hopefully motivate you to create the right circumstances to use deliberate practice long-term.

*Emotional support needs*

Support from others is another crucial aspect if you want to use deliberate practice long-term.

Doing deliberate practice can be tough on some days, especially at the beginning, when you are still figuring out this process.

At such times, it helps to have a strong support network that can cheer you on and keep you going despite all the difficulties you encounter.

Ask yourself if you have a strong enough support network to get you through the times of self-doubt that lie ahead.

If you find yourself lacking in this area, look for additional people you can ask for help, to give yourself the best chance of success.

. . .

*An accountability partner*

Using deliberate practice regularly is hard, and life gets in the way.

To keep your commitment, you may need an accountability partner–perhaps a fellow actor who is also working on their craft.

You could meet up with your accountability partner regularly, or check in occasionally in a more casual way.

In addition to keeping you accountable, you could also ask your accountability partner for feedback on whatever skill you are working on.

Your accountability partner may also be able to provide emotional support when needed, making you feel less alone on your journey with deliberate practice.

Having an accountability partner will likely take up some of your time, so you need to weigh up the pros and cons, but having someone like that by your side is worth considering.

## COMMITTING TO DELIBERATE PRACTICE

Take some time to think about the factors discussed in this chapter and anything else that feels relevant to you.

This will help you decide whether you can make a commitment to deliberate practice, or whether this is not something you can take on.

If you do not feel you can make space for deliberate practice in your life, it is better to be honest with yourself.

Alternatively, you may decide that you do want to commit to deliberate practice, but this is not the right time.

In that case, start thinking about what would need to change in your life to make space for taking on this extra commitment.

If you do decide to commit to deliberate practice, taking these factors into consideration will make it easier to keep going.

## KEY POINTS

- Applying deliberate practice to acting requires you to arrange your life in particular ways.
- Deliberate practice requires extra time, which means you may have to rework your existing schedule.
- You may need more sleep than usual, including naps during the day, because

of the high level of cognitive functioning that doing deliberate practice requires.

- Alternatively, you may need to do deliberate practice when you are at peak mental capacity during your day.
- Committing to deliberate practice may place financial constraints on you, such as having to arrange your bill-paying jobs around your deliberate practice sessions.
- You may need to call upon others for emotional support when you are going through a tough day and need some cheering up.
- You may also consider having an accountability partner to give yourself the best chance of success.

# CONCLUSION

Deliberate practice gives you a process to achieve excellence in anything you choose to improve.

There is no clear guidance specifically for actors, as there is for athletes or musicians.

Nevertheless, I hope this book has given you some ideas about how to apply deliberate practice to acting.

You now have a template for how to achieve excellence in your craft, something few actors have.

All you have to do is seize this opportunity and realize that you will get out of it what you put into it.

As you start using deliberate practice to improve specific aspects of your craft, it is important to give yourself time and patience.

You will need to experiment and see what works best for you. Getting to grips with deliberate practice takes time.

For example, if you have a strong inner critic, it is likely that, at the beginning, using deliberate practice will make you feel overly critical of yourself.

If so, remember to embrace the growth mindset when evaluating your progress.

That way, you will be glad when you find something that needs work, instead of feeling down about your mistakes.

At first, you may not notice when you are overly self-critical until you have already undermined your self-confidence.

This is natural, so do not beat yourself up over it.

Remind yourself that the purpose of the evaluation is to note what needs improving, not to make yourself feel bad.

The more you get into the habit of adopting a neutral stance and simply observing what your are doing, the better you will become at doing so, and the less your inner critic will interfere.

The growth mindset applies to deliberate practice as much as it applies to becoming better at anything else.

It is not about how "talented" you are at this type of practice; it is simply about trial and error, and getting better over time.

The fact that you have read this book to the end is already a step in the right direction.

Learning to use deliberate practice will put you miles ahead of where you are now.

It is worth pointing out that deliberate practice is a life skill.

As you learn to use deliberate practice in the context of your acting career, you will also start applying it to other areas of your life.

This process, and everything you will learn by using it, will not just make your acting career better–it will improve your life as a whole.

Remember that you are unique, so tailor the process of deliberate practice to your own needs.

Feel free to use the suggestions in this book as a starting point for developing your own process.

Finally, please consider passing on this knowledge to any actor friends who are serious about improving their craft.

They will benefit and be happier for it, and

you will become a beacon of strength and empowerment in their lives.

I wish you all the best with your acting career.

---

I would like to ask you for a small favor.

Reviews are the best way to spread the word about this book. If you have found this book helpful, it would mean a lot to me if you could leave a review.

Even if you write only a sentence or two, it will help. Thank you!

# A USEFUL RESOURCE

If you want to improve your chances of success as an actor, psychology can help.

*Psychology Tools for Actors* teaches you ten simple yet powerful psychology tools to take your acting career to the next level.

Download for free when you sign up for the *Psychology for Actors* newsletter at:

www.psychologyforactors.com/newsletter

## ABOUT THE AUTHOR

Alexa Ispas holds a PhD in psychology from the University of Edinburgh.

The books in her *Psychology for Actors Series* provide actors with proven psychology techniques to thrive and build a successful career.

If you'd like to stay in touch with Alexa and learn more psychological tools that are directly relevant to actors, please sign up for the *Psychology for Actors* newsletter. You will receive a short free book when you sign up.

You can sign up for the newsletter and receive your free book at:

www.psychologyforactors.com/newsletter

PSYCHOLOGY FOR ACTORS SERIES

Memorization for Actors

Self-Confidence for Actors

Resilience for Actors

Motivation for Actors

Excellence for Actors

Success for Actors

For more information, please visit:

www.psychologyforactors.com

Printed in Great Britain
by Amazon